BLACK
JACK

BLACK JACK

THE BALLAD OF JACK JOHNSON

CHARLES R. SMITH JR.
ILLUSTRATED BY
SHANE W. EVANS

A NEAL PORTER BOOK
ROARING BROOK PRESS
NEW YORK

To Jack, a man before his time.
And to Gillian, my beautiful partner in rhyme.—C.R.S. Jr.

Thank you God.
Dedicated to my father: a true fan of the sport of boxing.
Thank you for sharing the appreciation of the sport with me.—S.W.E.

Text copyright © 2010 by Charles R. Smith

Illustrations copyright © 2010 by Shane W. Evans

A Neal Porter Book

Published by Roaring Brook Press

Roaring Brook Press is a division of Holtzbrinck Publishing Holdings Limited Partnership

175 Fifth Avenue, New York, New York 10010

www.roaringbrookpress.com

Distributed in Canada by H. B. Fenn and Company Ltd.

Cataloging-in-Publication Data is on file at the Library of Congress

ISBN: 978-1-59643-473-8

Roaring Brook Press books are available for special promotions and premiums.

For details contact: Director of Special Markets, Holtzbrinck Publishers.

First Edition July 2010

Book design by Jennifer Browne

Printed in October 2009 in China by Macmillan Production (Asia) Ltd.,

Kwun Tong, Kowloon, Hong Kong (Supplier Code: 10)

1   3   5   7   9   8   6   4   2

Black Jack was a **brave** man.
Black Jack was a **STRONG** man.
Black Jack was a **brave**, STRONG,
FIGHTIN' man.
But mostly, Black Jack was his
OWN man.

"I am not a slave. Because
my ancestors came here
before anyone had
dreamed of a United States,
I consider myself
a pure-blooded **AMERICAN**."

Black Jack was born
Arthur John Johnson
in 1878, March thirty-one,
in the state of Texas,
in the city of Galveston.
Born to Henry and Tiny,
both former slaves,
Li'l Artha, as he was called,
wasn't always so brave.

Bullies **beat up** on young Jack
until he was **black** and **blue**.
His eyes were wet from crying.
He didn't know what to do.
His older sisters fought for him,
his mother's face was red,
until she wagged her finger
at him one day and said:

"JACK, FIGHT BACK!"

And fight Jack did,
beating all bullies
with two quick fists
thrown strong and surely.
Fighting, it seems,
came easy to Jack
and built up the confidence
he once sorely lacked.

Just **five years** of school
did young Jack attend,
but he loved to read stories
about great men.
Napoleon, the leader,
bike racer **Major Taylor**,
and jockey **Isaac Murphy**,
all inspired Jack's behavior—
inspired Jack to dream
of a life so grand,
inspired Jack to dream
of becoming a **great man**.

But it was words from his mother,
whom Jack loved so dear,
that Jack took to heart
when they entered his ear:

"Jack, you are the BEST boy
in the world. You can do
ANYTHING you want if
you want it badly enough."

What Jack wanted,
he didn't quite know,
but his mother kept at him
while he continued to
grow.

So, his curious **mind**
and his curious **body**,
worked plenty of jobs
to earn Jack money.

SHOP
SWEEPER

HORSE TRAINER

HOBO

PORTER

BOXER

With confident fists,
speed and agility,
Jack hopped freight trains
to test his ability.

Memphis, **Chicago**, and northeast to **Boston**,
out west to **California**, with stops back to **Galveston**,
Jack made a living using his fists,
won more than he lost and learned a few tricks.

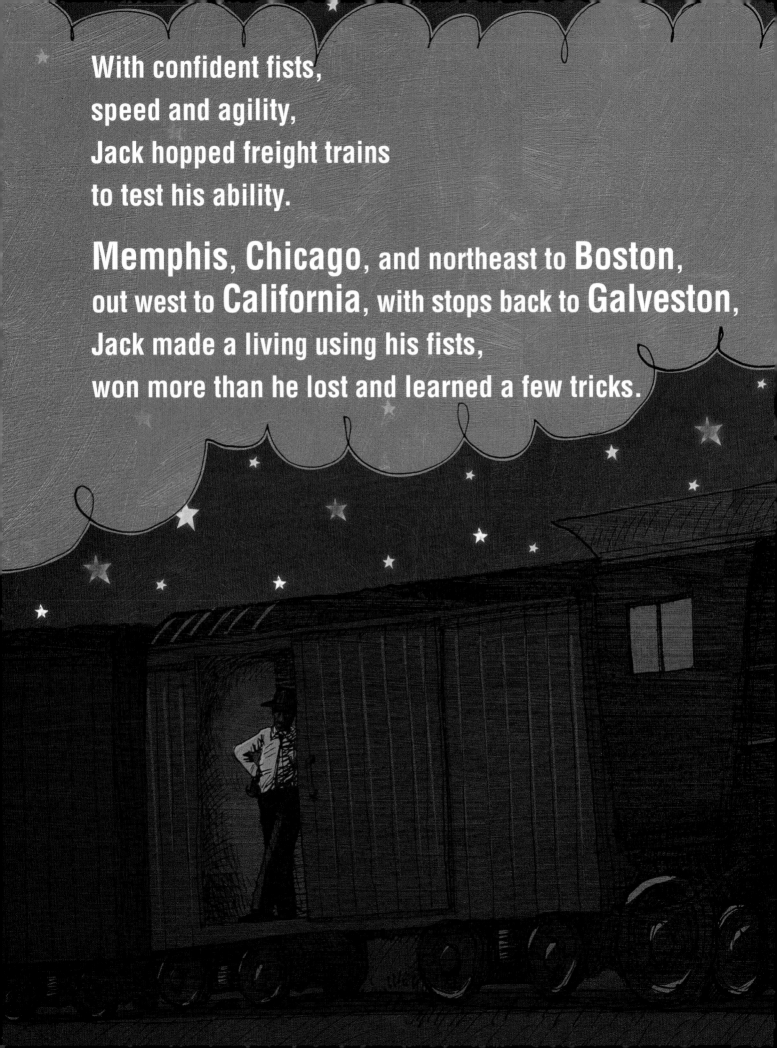

Nope, not many fists
touched Jack's chin,
but **his** touched plenty,
earning many a win.

Fast hands, a clever head,
reflexes like a cat,
and a big right uppercut
sent many to the mat.

With each fight fought
came new improved skills,
and with each win
came a fistful of bills.

With money in his pockets,
Jack showcased his style:
sharp suits, handsome hats,
and a bright, golden smile.

A sharp-dressed sport
with an even sharper mind,
Jack sometimes played bass
to relax and unwind.
He even invented a wrench
later on down the line.

A lover of cars,
Jack could often be found
flaunting his style
while tooling around town.

Behind the wheel of his car
Jack was just Jack,
but everywhere else,
Jack was just **black**.

Now, Jack was a **mighty** man,
and Jack was a *fightin'* man,
and Jack was a ***MIGHTY, FIGHTIN'*** man.

But what Jack wanted most
was to be a **great** man,
so he challenged the times.
But it was Jack who was challenged
when he faced the **color** line.

White only fought white
and that kept Jack out
of the ring, to fight the champ
in a championship bout.

on Says "He Will Fight Anyone They Put In The Ring"!

"I will never fight a Negro."
—Jim Jeffries, heavyweight champ

So Jack chased the champ
from fight to fight,
challenging Jim Jeffries
to prove his might.

Jack wanted to prove
he was the best fighter,
but instead of fighting Jack,
Jim Jeffries retired.

With the title up for grabs,
Jack now had a chance
to break the color line
with his **mighty,**
fightin' hands.

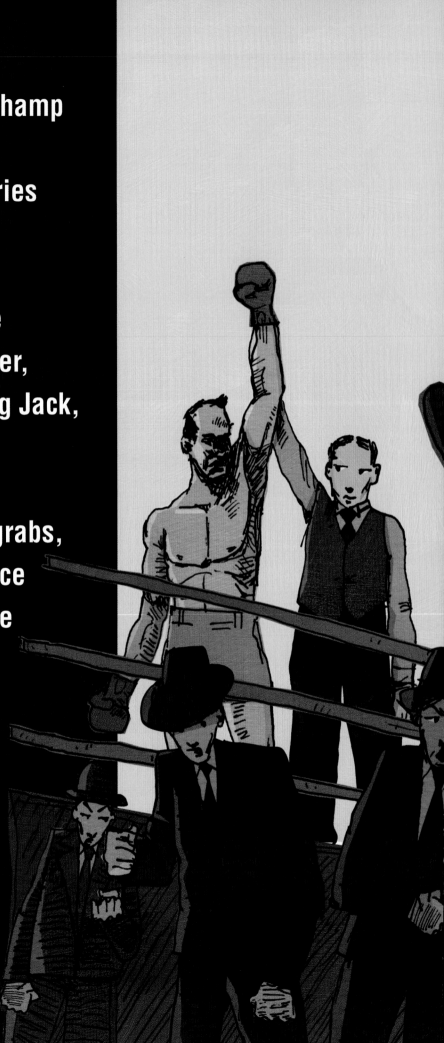

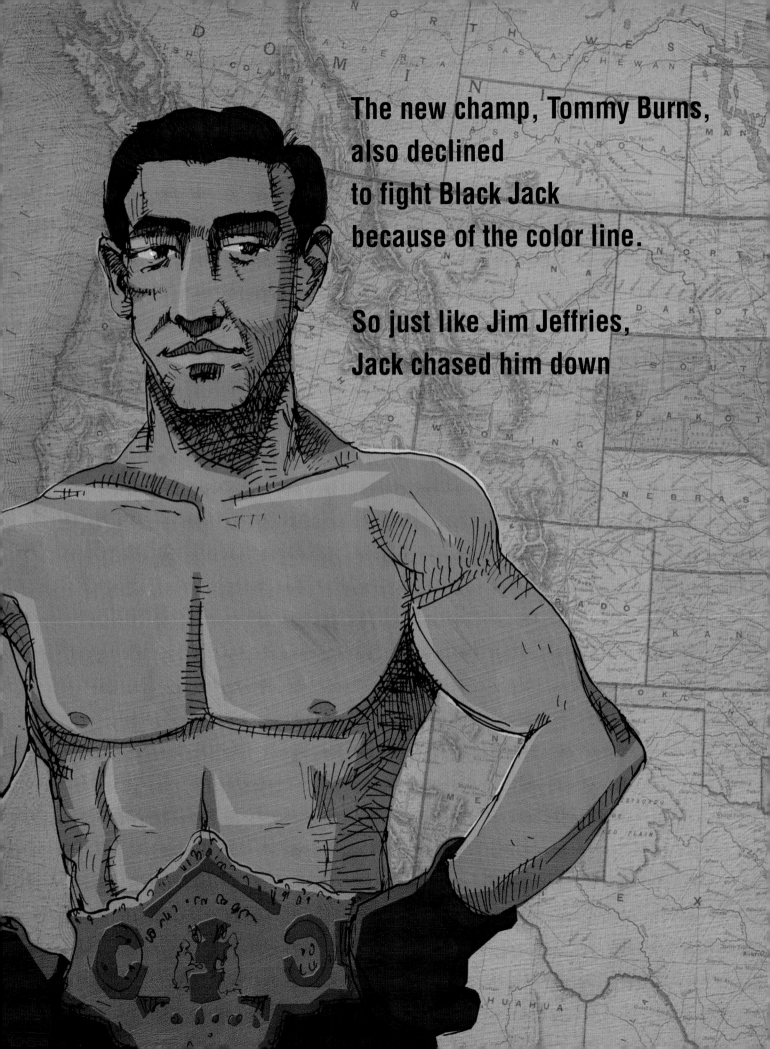

The new champ, Tommy Burns, also declined to fight Black Jack because of the color line.

So just like Jim Jeffries, Jack chased him down

from city to city
to contend for the crown.

From **San Fran** to **New York**,
to **Paris** to **London**,
for two years, Jack
was a man on a mission.

At long last,
Tommy stepped into the ring
to battle Black Jack
for a mountain of green.

**Rushcutters Bay,
Australia**, was the scene
for the black and white battle
to crown boxing's biggest king.

Thousands filled the stadium
as well as the surrounding trees
hoping "Tommy Boy"
would knock Jack to his knees.

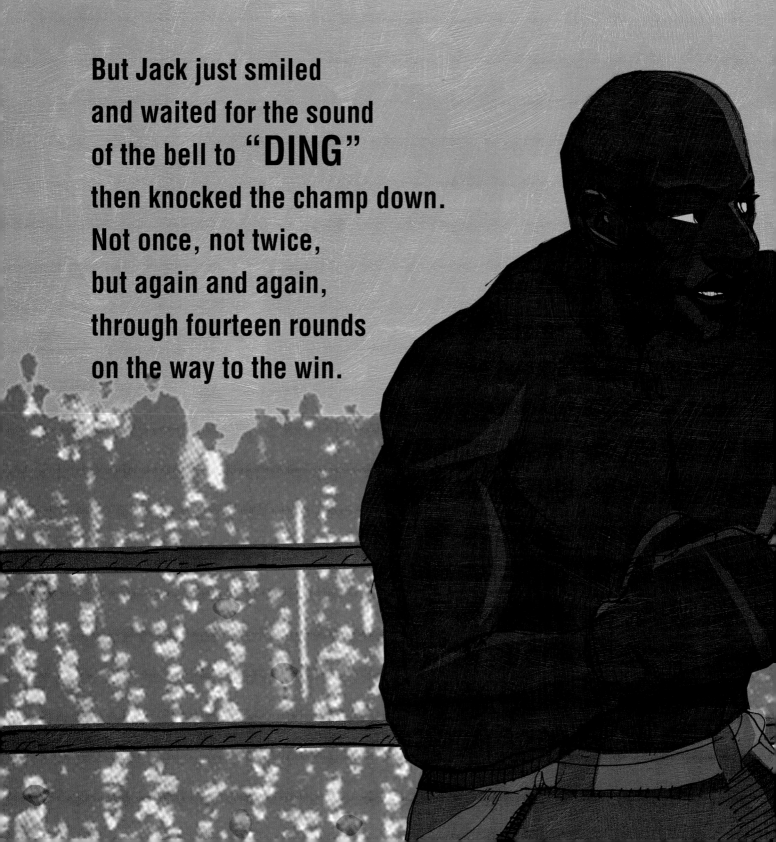

When Jack rose in the ring
a sea of white faces
turned a battle of **men**
to a battle of **races**.

But Jack just smiled
and waited for the sound
of the bell to **"DING"**
then knocked the champ down.
Not once, not twice,
but again and again,
through fourteen rounds
on the way to the win.

Fans in the stands
sat wide-eyed and surprised,
but black faces back home
beamed with pride.

Jack was now champ,
but in less than a day,
voices worldwide
spoke up to say: "BURNS WASN'T THE
                    REAL CHAMP ANYWAY."
"BURNS WAS JUST A NEWSPAPER
CHAMP."   "BURNS NEVER FOUGHT
JIM JEFFRIES."   "JEFFRIES
RETIRED UNDEFEATED, SO
UNTIL SOMEBODY BEATS HIM,
HE'S STILL THE CHAMP."   "JIM,
COME OUT OF RETIREMENT
AND WIPE THAT SMILE OFF
JOHNSON'S FACE. YOU'RE
OUR ONLY HOPE."

But Jim wouldn't budge
until eighteen months later,
when he and Jack stood
surrounded by spectators
in a ring in Reno,
Nevada, to see
who was the champ in
"THE BATTLE OF THE CENTURY."

On the fourth of July,
in 1910,
on a clear desert day
stood two mighty men.
Jack versus Jim,
one black, one white,
two mighty, fightin' men,
ready to fight.

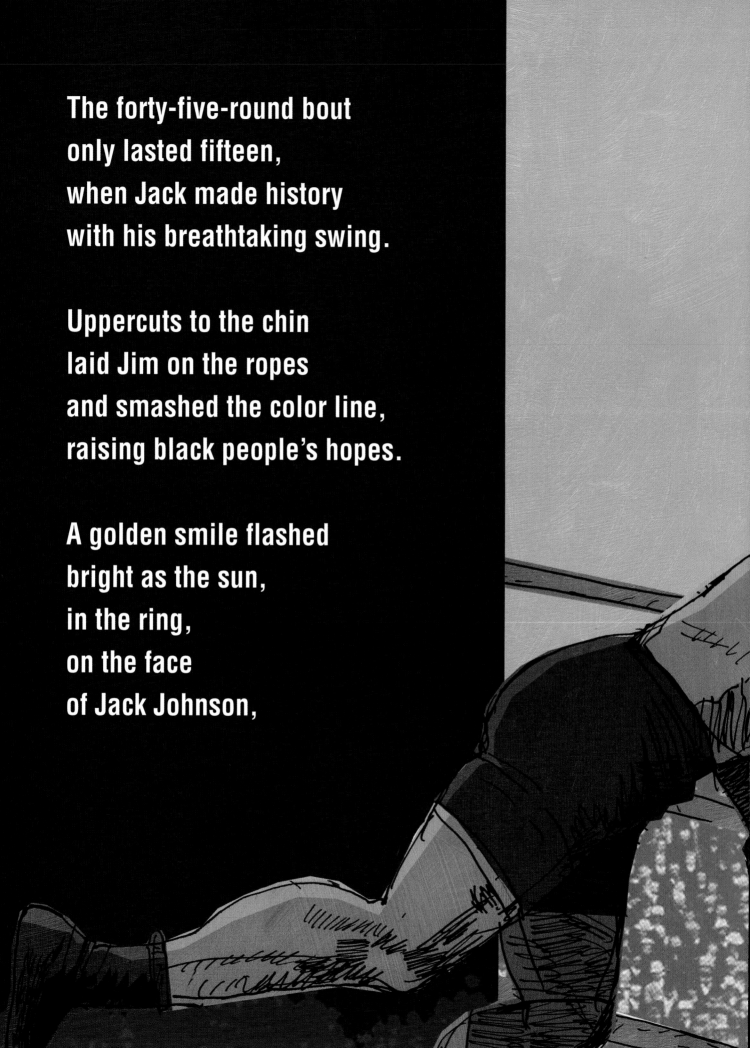

The forty-five-round bout
only lasted fifteen,
when Jack made history
with his breathtaking swing.

Uppercuts to the chin
laid Jim on the ropes
and smashed the color line,
raising black people's hopes.

A golden smile flashed
bright as the sun,
in the ring,
on the face
of Jack Johnson,

THE WORLD'S FIRST
BLACK
HEAVYWEIGHT
CHAMPION!

"AND THEN WHAT HAPPENED?"

JACK JOHNSON was a complex man living in a difficult time. He was born free, unlike his parents, and demanded to be treated as such. He had no use for anyone who treated him poorly because of the color of his skin. When he wanted to buy a nice house in a white neighborhood, his manager tried to talk him out of it because he thought Jack was "getting too big for his britches." Jack fired him on the spot. Nobody told Jack Johnson what to do!

And that was the problem. A black man like Jack, who dressed in the most expensive clothes and drove the nicest cars, posed a threat to many people, so they did whatever they could to "keep him in his place." In November, 1912 he was arrested for dating a woman outside of his race, under a newly created law called the Mann Act. He served one week in prison before being released on bail. Once his case went to court in May, 1913, he was convicted and sentenced to a year and a day in federal prison but soon left the country to escape imprisonment, returning in 1920 to serve his sentence. It was during his time in jail that he invented, and patented, a wrench for tightening loosened fastenings.

Jack lost his title to Jess Willard in Havana, Cuba, 1915, but continued to fight professionally until 1938.

After retiring from boxing, Jack earned a living by performing in vaudeville shows, showing his boxing skills, telling stories, and signing autographs. A new black heavyweight champion, Joe Louis, was on the horizon and Jack, retired but confident as ever, announced that he could have easily whipped the new champ.

Jack would die behind the wheel of his car shortly after that statement on June 9, 1946, when he zoomed around a sharp curve, swerved to avoid an oncoming truck, then slammed into a telephone pole.

At his funeral, 2,500 people filled the church while thousands stood outside mourning the loss of a man who died as he lived; fearless and free.

BIBLIOGRAPHY

Ward, Geoffrey C. *Unforgivable Blackness: The Rise and Fall of Jack Johnson*. Vintage, 2006.

Unforgivable Blackness: The Rise and Fall of Jack Johnson, DVD, directed by Ken Burns. PBS, 2004.

Jakoubek, Robert. *Jack Johnson* (Black Americans of Achievement series). Chelsea House, 1990.

Johnson, Jack and Rivers, Christopher. *My Life and Battles: By Jack Johnson*. Praeger, 2007.

Davis, Miles. *A Tribute to Jack Johnson*, CD, Sony Records, 1970.